Cool STEAM Careers

FBI SPECIAL AGENT

WIL MARA

Published in the United States of America by Cherry Lake Publishing
Ann Arbor, Michigan
www.cherrylakepublishing.com

Content Adviser: law enforcement members
Reading Adviser: Marla Conn, ReadAbility, Inc.

Photo Credits: ©DmitriMaruta/Shutterstock Images, cover, 1 ; © Frances M. Roberts/Alamy, 5; © Richard Cavalleri/
Shutterstock Images, 6; © kilukilu/Shutterstock Images, 9; © Bliznetsov/iStock Images, 10, 29; © Simone van den
Berg/Shutterstock Images, 12; © Robert Ingelhart/iStockphoto, 15; © bikeriderlondon/Shutterstock Images, 16;
© Christopher Futcher/iStockphoto, 17; © LukaTDB/Shutterstock Images, 18; © Yuri_Arcurs/iStock Images, 21;
© Stockbyte/Thinkstock Images, 22; © MATTHEW HEALEY/UPI/Newscom, 25; © Andrey_Popov/Shutterstock
Images, 26

Library of Congress Cataloging-in-Publication Data

Mara, Wil.
 FBI special agent/Wil Mara.
    pages cm.—(Cool STEAM careers)
 Includes index.
 ISBN 978-1-63362-558-7 (hardcover)—ISBN 978-1-63362-738-3 (pdf)—ISBN 978-1-63362-648-5 (pbk.)—
ISBN 978-1-63362-828-1 (ebook)
 1. United States. Federal Bureau of Investigation—Juvenile literature. 2. Law enforcement—
United States—Juvenile literature. I. Title.

 HV8144.F43M37 2016
 363.25023'73—dc23
                          2015005359

Cherry Lake Publishing would like to acknowledge the work of
the Partnership for 21st Century Skills. Please visit *www.p21.org*
for more information.

Printed in the United States of America
Corporate Graphics

ABOUT THE AUTHOR

Wil Mara is an award-winning and best-selling author of more than 150 books, many of which
are educational titles for young readers. Further information about his work can be found at
www.wilmara.com.

TABLE OF CONTENTS

STEAM is the acronym for Science, Technology, Engineering, Arts, and Mathematics. In this book, you will read about how each of these study areas is connected to a career in the Federal Bureau of Investigation.

THE BUREAU

Cameras flash as a handcuffed man is escorted out of a courtroom. He has just been charged with a federal crime. Dozens of reporters want to talk to him. FBI special agents escort him to a van. They're transporting him from the courtroom to prison. He'll be in federal **custody** until his trial is over. He was one of the most wanted criminals in the nation, and these agents were responsible for bringing him to justice.

FBI stands for Federal Bureau of Investigation. It is the main agency of the U.S. government that investigates over 200 types of federal crimes, or crimes that break laws

The FBI deals with criminals who have broken federal laws.

passed by the U.S. Congress. They include bank robbery, kidnapping, and **terrorism**. The FBI doesn't investigate crimes that violate state or local laws, like speeding, shoplifting, and most murders. State and local police handle those.

In 1908, Attorney General Charles Bonaparte hired investigators to work for the Department of Justice. This small group of former detectives and **Secret Service** agents was called the special agents force. They became known as the Federal Bureau of Investigation in 1935.

The headquarters office of the FBI is named after one of its founders, J. Edgar Hoover.

One main reason the FBI was needed was because criminals had started committing crimes while traveling, since improvements in trains and cars were making transportation easier. In those early days, the FBI mostly handled bank robberies. These were common in the 1930s because many Americans were still feeling the crush of the Great Depression.

In the 1950s, Congress passed many new laws that turned more crimes into federal offenses. Since then the FBI's role has evolved as well. In 1968, the FBI received permission to conduct **wiretaps** under certain circumstances. This helped them catch members of **organized crime** groups, and other criminals. The Patriot Act of 2001 expanded the FBI's role in preventing terrorism.

Today, the FBI employs more than 30,000 people. It has more than 12,000 special agents. The bureau's headquarters are located in Washington, D.C. The FBI also has more than 400 offices, which are located in smaller U.S. cities and in foreign countries. The FBI is one of the most respected law enforcement agencies in the world.

THINK ABOUT ART

Those who want to work as FBI special agents will benefit greatly if they can think creatively, as artists do. Fighting crime has certain scientific aspects, but criminals rarely act in predictable ways. (If they did, they'd be very easy to catch.) Thus, a smart agent has to learn to think outside the box and find creative ways to outsmart their opponents.

CHAPTER 2

CATCHING THE BAD GUYS

The FBI's job is to investigate violations of federal laws. Whenever there's a bank robbery or a kidnapping, local police call in the FBI. The bureau also investigates all violations of national security, including spying by foreign governments. While there's no doubt that working as an FBI special agent can be exciting and rewarding, it can also be fairly dangerous.

Since the 9/11 attacks, the FBI has helped protect the United States from further incidents of terrorism. The FBI also helps law enforcement agencies in other

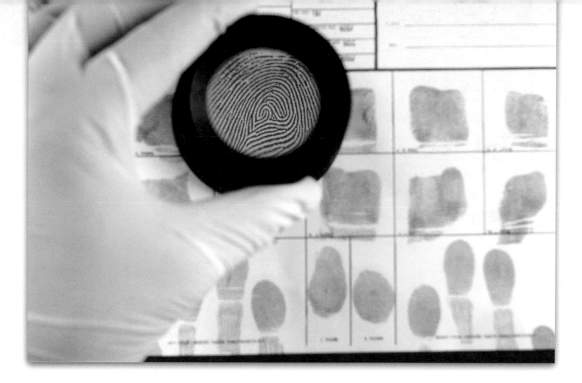

The FBI keeps many fingerprints on record.

countries that are allies by allowing access to its resources, such as fingerprint identifications and laboratory testing. It also offers advanced training in everything from weapons usage to computer technology.

Each agent has many responsibilities. An agent spends a lot of time in the field investigating crimes. Field investigations involve examining crime scenes and interviewing witnesses. Agents review business and public records. They work with crime-lab technicians and other experts to help analyze evidence. They may follow

Some FBI agents conduct stakeouts to monitor suspected criminals.

and watch suspects for days, weeks, and even months at a time. Sometimes they go **undercover**, which is a little like putting on a costume and pretending that you're somebody else. And while this might sound like fun, it can be very risky.

Special agents investigate many different types of crime, including major thefts. These include bank robberies, art thefts, and jewelry thefts. They also handle cases involving kidnapping, major crimes on Native American reservations, and crimes committed aboard airplanes and cruise ships. They investigate **identity theft** cases and white-collar crimes. White-collar crimes are committed by business and government professionals. These crimes include corporate **fraud**, insurance fraud, and telemarketing fraud.

Special agents also investigate three other types of crime. **Cybercrimes** are crimes in which computers or the Internet play a key role in the illegal activity. **Hacking** and copyright violations are two common

THINK ABOUT SCIENCE

FBI investigations rely on numerous branches of science —toxicology, forensics, acoustics, and biology, to name a few. Fighting crime would be nearly impossible if we didn't know how to examine DNA, determine cause of death, and lift fingerprints. If you dream of being a special agent someday, you should study as many of the sciences used in crime fighting as possible. High school classes in biology, chemistry, and physics would be a great start.

FBI agents have to work long hours, and often find themselves in places other than at a desk.

types of cybercrime. Organized crime activities include the illegal sale of guns and drugs, sports bribery, and murder. Civil rights crimes include hate crimes (crimes against a person or property that are motivated by someone's prejudice against an aspect of the victim's identity, such as his or her race or religion) and certain criminal acts committed by government officials.

A special agent's job is difficult, exciting, and rewarding. Agents often work long hours. They spend a lot of time away from their offices and families. They are always connected with smartphones and tablets. They are required to be available every hour of every day. The job is never boring!

CHAPTER 3

BECOMING AN FBI SPECIAL AGENT

The FBI is very selective. Tens of thousands of people apply to be a special agent every year, but only several hundred are hired. The bureau has certain requirements involving age, education, and physical fitness.

To become a special agent, you must be between the ages of 23 and 36 and have a four-year college degree and a valid driver's license. You must pass both a physical fitness test and a medical examination, which includes vision and hearing tests. You also have to pass a drug-screening test and a lie detector. Male

FBI candidates need to be in top physical shape.

candidates must be registered with the **Selective Service System**.

FBI candidates go through several tests and interviews. The bureau conducts a thorough background check of each candidate's life. This means you must allow the FBI to talk to your friends, family, romantic partners, bosses, neighbors, teachers, and others. They will check your school and work records. They will also make sure you don't have a criminal record.

FBI special agents come from many different academic backgrounds. Each of these is a separate career path that the

A background in law, accounting, foreign languages, or technology will look good on a job application for the FBI.

FBI recommends:

1. Law: a law degree from an accredited law school

2. Accounting: a college degree in business or accounting, and a license as a Certified Public Accountant

3. Languages: a college degree, plus proven ability in at least one foreign language (preferably Arabic, Chinese, Farsi, Russian, Spanish, and/or Vietnamese)

4. Information technology: a degree in computer science, information technology, or electrical

People with extremely strong computer skills might be able to work as FBI agents.

The FBI sometimes investigates murders.

engineering; or certification as an IT professional

5. Diversified: a college degree plus three years of work experience; or an advanced degree plus two years of work experience

At the end of the application process, the FBI will inform you of its hiring decision. If you are accepted as a special agent trainee, you will spend 20 weeks training at the FBI Academy in Quantico, Virginia. You will have to take courses on how to interview witnesses, question suspects, and evaluate evidence. You will learn how to defend yourself and protect others, sometimes with firearms. The special agent program also involves physical training.

THINK ABOUT ENGINEERING

Engineering is the art of building things, and a smart FBI special agent builds a case against criminals the same way a structural engineer builds a bridge or a building—one brick at a time. Every bit of evidence you gather moves you closer to breaking a case and catching the responsible parties. The more bricks you can stack, the stronger your case will be.

ON THE JOB

After finishing the training program, the trainee will be sworn in as a special agent. During the first two years on the job, new agents must show that they can use the basic skills they've just learned. They also receive on-the-job training from more experienced special agents, which gives them the kind of real-life experience they cannot get anywhere else. It helps them begin to develop the kind of **streetwise** instincts that can only come from real situations. There is no greater teacher than experience.

Some FBI agents have dogs to help them locate clues.

New agents may face many challenges. They must agree to serve for three years. Agents are often required to relocate to different offices. They are often working at strange hours, sometimes needing to sleep all day and work all night. Undercover agents sometimes have to disguise themselves. They might wear uncomfortable clothes, wear special-effects makeup, or even speak in fake accents. An agent has to be very good at taking on a new personality, because his or her safety will be at stake. All of this can make the new job difficult.

Some police officers use the skills they learned in the police force to become FBI agents.

FBI agents often stay in this profession for many years. In fact, not counting those who retire, only 4 percent of all special agents leave the FBI each year. Agents can retire between the ages of 57 and 65, depending on the situation, or after 20 years on the job. The agent will still be young enough to pursue other interests if he or she wants to.

Using the skills they learned in the FBI, many retired agents go into a different line of work. They might work at laboratories, teach classes, become attorneys, or work in private security. They can also give advice to a variety of nongovernment organizations and projects.

THINK ABOUT TECHNOLOGY

Criminals use technology just like everyone else. Every advancement that helps the rest of us helps them, too. The most successful FBI agents will need to be aware of all the cutting-edge technological developments in order to stay a step ahead of the bad guys. The main advantage the agents have is that they work for the federal government—the very place where a lot of these incredible technologies are born.

CHAPTER 5

THE FUTURE OF THE SPECIAL AGENT

The duties of an FBI special agent have changed over time because the nature of crime has also changed. Agents in the future will face new and different challenges we can't even imagine now.

Advances in transportation and communication have forever altered the way countries connect with one another. This trend, known as **globalization**, will continue to increase the flow of information around the world. And while there are advantages to this, it will also allow criminals more opportunities to commit crimes.

There is little doubt we will see increased threats from international crime organizations. As a result, more of the FBI's work will take place abroad. So the bureau will have a greater need for special agents with foreign language skills and deep knowledge of foreign cultures.

The FBI expects that terrorist groups will cooperate with one another more in the future. In addition,

The FBI evacuated residents of Cambridge, Massachusetts, during the manhunt for the Boston Marathon bomber in April 2013.

In recent years, the amount of cybercrime has grown quickly.

information about building nuclear and biological weapons has become easier to obtain. The bureau and similar agencies will have to make certain that violent terrorist groups don't get their hands on these weapons.

Cybercrimes will also increase in the future, which means people will be more at risk for crimes like identity theft. The FBI also believes that public corruption cases will increase in the future. For example, government spending is expected to increase (it almost always does). That means there will be more opportunities for government officials to use a portion of those funds fraudulently.

A career as an FBI agent can be exciting, challenging, and rewarding. It requires a lot of education, good physical fitness, and a desire to serve your country. If you think you can live up to the bureau's motto—Fidelity, Bravery, and Integrity—then you should learn all you can about becoming an FBI agent.

THINK ABOUT MATH

Mary Ellen O'Toole, PhD, a retired FBI profiler, often used reasoning and logic when trying to narrow down criminal suspects. She says, "My job did not require advanced algebra or differential equations. It required logic and reasoning and both were applied to real life—real crimes and real people. That breathed a lot of life into math for me and made it exciting."

The FBI offers many other career opportunities, many of which help special agents do their jobs more effectively. Scientists in the FBI crime labs analyze evidence. Computer specialists provide information technology and forensic analysis assistance. Intelligence analysts help investigators through analysis of documents and reports related to spying and terrorism cases. Language specialists translate documents and help conduct witness interviews. Remember, solving crimes often requires different people with different skills all working together.

Some scientists work for the FBI by analyzing fingerprints, which is sometimes key to solving a case.

THINK ABOUT IT

Most FBI agents move on to other jobs when they turn 57 years old. Why do you think that is? What would some of the challenges be for an FBI agent older than that?

Go online with an adult to find out how you can protect yourself (and your computer) from cyber-crimes. There are lots of simple steps that even kids can take. Which things do you do already? Which things should you start doing?

Look online to find a historical case that the FBI handled, such as the Lindbergh baby kidnapping (1932) or the Wall Street bombing (1920). How did the agents' actions compare to the techniques discussed in this book? How might new technology used today have helped them?

LEARN MORE

FURTHER READING

Labrecque, Ellen. *Fighting Crime*. Chicago: Raintree, 2012.

Snedden, Robert. *Crime-Fighting Devices*. Chicago: Raintree, 2011.

Thomas, William David. *How to Become an FBI Agent*. Broomhall, PA: Mason Crest Publishers, 2014.

Zullo, Allan. *10 True Tales: FBI Heroes*. New York: Scholastic Publishing, 2014.

WEB SITES

Federal Bureau of Investigation—Careers
www.fbijobs.gov
Learn more about working for the FBI.

Federal Bureau of Investigation—Kids Page
www.fbi.gov/fbikids.htm
Find out more about the FBI through games, tips, and stories.

GLOSSARY

custody (KUHS-tuh-dee) the legal right to supervise a suspect (by a law enforcement authority) or a child (by an adult)

cybercrimes (SYE-ber-krimez) crimes committed over the Internet

fraud (FRAWD) the intentional use of dishonesty to gain money or property illegally

globalization (glohb-uhl-uh-ZAY-shuhn) the growth of international economic activity, which includes increased movement of goods, money, and people between countries

hacking (HAK-ing) illegally accessing someone else's computer system to destroy, disrupt, or commit a crime

identity theft (eye-DEN-ti-tee THEFT) when someone uses another person's personal information, such as their name or credit card number, to commit a crime

organized crime (OR-guh-nized KRIME) crimes committed by a large group of people, such as a gang, who work together to profit from illegal activity

Secret Service (SEE-krit SUR-viss) a federal law enforcement agency that protects national and visiting government leaders and investigates some federal crimes

Selective Service System (si-LEK-tiv SUR-viss SIS-tuhm) a federal government program in which young men provide contact information in case they are needed in the military in a time of war

streetwise (STREET-wize) having the skills and experience needed to survive in a difficult or dangerous, usually urban, environment

terrorism (TER-uh-riz-uhm) violence or threats used in order to frighten people, obtain power, and/or force a government to do something

undercover (uhn-dur-KUHV-ur) posing as a criminal or other person to get information about a suspect or gather evidence about a crime

wiretaps (WIRE-taps) the act of using devices that allow law enforcement agents to gather information by listening in on telephone and other conversations

INDEX